W9-DFQ-848

# Zak at the Fair

Story by Maribeth Boelts

Illustrations by Nikki Boetger

It was the afternoon of the neighborhood fair. Zak and Sofie were excited.

"I smell popcorn!" said Zak.

"Me, too," said Sofie. "Let's play games, and then have some."

FAIR

TODAY

Zak played the "Ring Toss" game first.
He threw blue and green rings,
but they bounced off the bottles.
Then, he tossed a red ring.

SUPER
BOWLING

The red ring landed on a bottle.

"You won," said a neighbor, handing Zak a ticket. "You can trade your tickets for prizes."

At the prize table, Zak saw a paint set with 24 colors.

"I need to win ten tickets to get this paint set," said Zak.

"I need to win seven tickets for the jump rope," said Sofie.

"We can do it," said Zak.
"Let's go play some more games."

They went to the "Shape Walk" game.

"When the music ends, stop on a shape," a neighbor explained. "If I call your shape, you'll win a ticket."

Zak marched around the circle.
When the music ended, he stopped
on a square.

"Triangle," called the neighbor.

Zak played again. This time he stopped on a rectangle.

"Rectangle," called the neighbor, and Zak earned one ticket.

Next, Zak visited the "Pop-the-Balloon" game. If he popped the red balloon, he'd win three tickets.

When it was Zak's turn,
a neighbor handed him
four darts. Zak popped a
purple balloon, a yellow balloon,
and a blue balloon, while
Sofie cheered.

Zak had one dart left.

"Ready, aim, throw!" he said.
Zak's last dart flew through the air.

POP

"Three more tickets!
That makes five altogether!"
said Zak.

Just then, Kit and Piper walked by with a bag of popcorn and a green snow cone.

"Let's have some snacks," said Sofie. "I'll get the popcorn."

At the snack stand, Zak asked
for a green snow cone.

"We're out of green," said the neighbor.
"Is there another color you'd like?"

Zak remembered mixing yellow and blue to make green.

"What if you mixed yellow and blue?" Zak asked.

"Let's try it," said the neighbor, as she poured the colors together.

"It worked! Yellow and blue made green," Zak said. "Thank you!"

Then Zak asked for an orange
snow cone for Sofie.

"Red and yellow mixed together make
orange," Zak said.

As Zak and Sofie were eating, Zak saw some friends picking their prizes.

"I have seven tickets for the jump rope," said Sofie. "How many tickets do you have?"

"I have five," Zak said. "I need five more to make ten. I just hope no one picks the paint set before I win them."

Zak walked over to a "Beanbag Toss" game he hadn't played yet.

"I win one ticket if I throw a beanbag through a circle," Zak said, "and two tickets if I throw one through the diamond."

Zak aimed and tossed a beanbag.
It missed the diamond and bounced off.
Zak tossed another beanbag.
This one flew through the diamond.

Beanbag Toss
● 1 ticket
◆ 2 tickets

"I won two more tickets,"
said Zak.
"Now, I have seven."

Zak's friends began leaving the fair.

"The fair is ending," a neighbor said.
"Choose your last game."

Zak hurried to the "Super Bowling" game.

"I can win a ticket for every pin I knock down," Zak said.

He rolled the ball toward the pins.

"Come on, Zak!" Sofie cheered.

Three pins wobbled,
but only one fell over.
Zak won his last ticket.

"Eight tickets isn't enough," Zak said sadly.
"I'll have to choose a different prize."

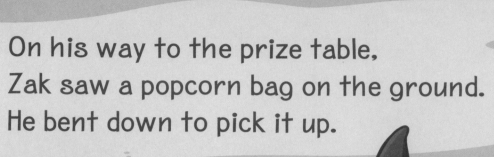

On his way to the prize table,
Zak saw a popcorn bag on the ground.
He bent down to pick it up.

TRASH

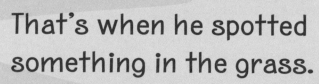

That's when he spotted
something in the grass.

"A ticket!" said Zak.

"Look, Zak!" Sofie said. "It's folded together. It's not just one ticket—it's two!"

Zak counted his tickets one last time.
"I have ten tickets!" he exclaimed.
"Now I can get the paint set!"

Zak smiled. "This was a fun day at the fair."

purple

red

blue

orange

green

yellow

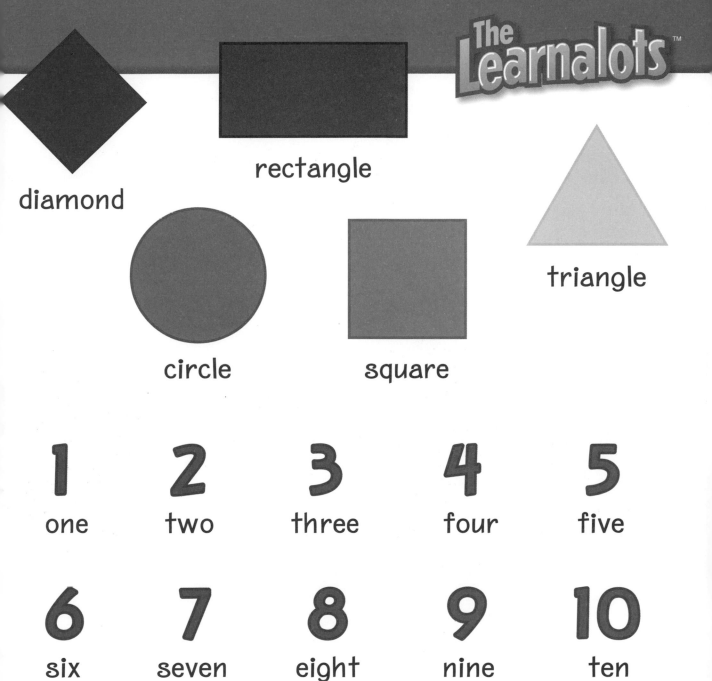

diamond

rectangle

triangle

circle

square

**1** one

**2** two

**3** three

**4** four

**5** five

**6** six

**7** seven

**8** eight

**9** nine

**10** ten

# The Learnalots™

**Bo**
Literacy

**Kit**
Math

**Piper**
Music and Movement

**Sofie**
Social and Emotional Sk

**Flora**
Nature

**Scout**
Health and Fitness

**Leo**
Science

**Zak**
Art and Creativity

**BrightStart Learning**
7342 11th Ave. NW
Seattle, WA 98117
www.brightstartlearning.com

Developed in conjunction with Trillium Publishing, Inc.

Illustrations created by Nikki Boet

ISBN: 978-1-938751-05-9

Printed and bound in China.

10  9  8  7  6  5  4  3  2  1